AMANDA LECAUDÉ

LIFE SKILLS HANDBOOK

Conquering Time Management and Organisation

Dedication

To my family and friends, who continue to encourage me to learn and grow in support of others.

To my students, thank you for your ongoing inspiration, ideas and reminders of why I do what I do – making a difference to your lives! It is a pleasure to be part of your life's journey.

Acknowledgements

I would like to thank the following people for their support, guidance and education in the early years of my career in working with students: Kathy Jenkins, Ellen Delap, Leslie Josel, Ellen Faye and Gretchen Wagner. Each and every one of you has influenced – either directly or indirectly – the path I have chosen with my business and why I do what I do today in supporting students.

There are also many others – too many to list and name, although you will know who you are! A very big thank you for also being part of my journey.

Published in 2024 by Amba Press, Melbourne, Australia
www.ambapress.com.au

© Amanda Lecaudé 2024

All rights reserved. No part of this book may be reproduced or transmitted in any form or by any means, electronic or mechanical, including photocopying, recording or by any information storage and retrieval system, without prior permission in writing from the publisher.

Cover design: Tess McCabe
Editor: Rica Dearman

ISBN: 9781923116672 (pbk)
ISBN: 9781923116689 (ebk)

A catalogue record for this book is available from the National Library of Australia.

Contents

Introduction		1
Chapter 1	Understanding time	5
Chapter 2	Managing time	9
Chapter 3	What does it mean to be organised?	17
Chapter 4	What role does organisation play?	21
Chapter 5	How planning tools can help	29
Chapter 6	The importance of planning	35
Chapter 7	Being effective and productive	41
Chapter 8	Managing procrastination and distractions	49
Chapter 9	Completing tasks to the best of your ability	57
Chapter 10	Being a good self-advocate	61
Chapter 11	The feedback loop	67
Chapter 12	Additional learning challenges	71
Chapter 13	Independence and self-management	77

Introduction

Every day, organisation and time management have implications for every single one of us. As a result of this, it is important to understand what is meant by each of these terms, how they impact and constantly intertwine with each other in our lives, and how, as a student, you can best manage them to work for you.

Ever since my boys were in primary school (they are both now adults), it has been a goal of mine to educate and provide tools and strategies to students to develop skills in both organisation and time management in order for them to succeed at both school and in life. Therefore, I have written this book to assist you now with your journey at secondary school as well as into the future, wherever life might take you.

Defining organisation and time management

Here are some thoughts from Year 6 and 7 students on what these key words actually mean:

Organisation – helpful, neat, tidy, prepared, ready, having a plan, knowing what to do, knowing where things are, being able to fit tasks in, process, a group of people, being organised, having things sorted, knowing what order to do something, having things in a place to make them easy to find, being able to find things, having time, colour coding, a place for everything, thinking ahead.

Time management – planning, schedule, timetable, prioritising, knowing what and when, knowing what is important to be doing, knowing how to use time, being aware of what to do, meeting deadlines, having a plan of action, managing time, limited time, not wasting time, using time wisely, not procrastinating, being on time, spacing time across different activities or things, using a planner, having balance, being on task, being focused, being efficient.

Can you relate to any of the following right now?

- You wish you had more free time or you seem to have a lot of free time and rush to get your work done.
- You are unsure of what homework needs to be completed and when it is due.
- You seem to be overwhelmed, get anxious and are not sure where to start.
- You struggle with time and the management of a student planner/diary/planning tool or don't use anything at all.
- You work late into the night before a task is due in order to complete it.
- You sometimes or regularly miss project/assignment deadlines.

- You have a cluttered and disorganised desk or bedroom space.
- You forget you have a test, assessment or a piece of work to hand in.
- You have a school bag or locker full of 'stuff', the contents of which is largely unknown to you.
- You have piles of papers and notes that don't appear to be organised in any way.
- You spend a lot of time looking for information.
- You forget to hand in schoolwork.
- You get distracted easily and/or procrastinate.
- You are always running late for school, activities or events.
- You need to be reminded by parents regularly about events, homework and things that need to be done for school.

If you resonate with any or many of the above points, then this book has been written with you in mind. Many students – and also people of all ages – struggle to be organised or manage their time, so you are not alone in this space if any of the above sounds like you.

You will already have many tools in your toolbox, and this book is designed to give you a few more. So, take a read, and as you do, I encourage you to take notice of the key tools and strategies to keep front and centre in order to help you navigate school and life.

While the focus of this book is primarily on school, most of what is mentioned will also assist you in the future, whether that be via further studies or into the workforce once you finish secondary school.

Keep an open mind when reading, and use this as an opportunity to both learn new skills and refresh your current knowledge and skills.

But before you continue to read, take a moment to think and reflect on what is or isn't working for you at present when it comes to your own organisation and time management. Once you have had a moment to reflect, read on to find out how this book can help you.

This book will contain some things that you will already be great at, and others that you are either not doing or might not even be aware of. So, as you read, think about the areas that are likely to help you. From there, armed with those areas to work on, you can take the next step and have a go at putting them into practice.

Remember, it is important to keep in mind that you shouldn't try to put everything into practice at the same time – I suggest that you pick one or two things to focus on to start with, and then build from there.

Ultimately, your goal is to use these skills to have balance across all aspects of your life: school, home, sport and other activities you enjoy.

Thank you for the opportunity to support you now and into your future.

CHAPTER 1

Understanding time

First and foremost, it is important to really understand what time means and how it impacts your day-to-day life as a student.

In an ideal world, it would be great if time was infinite and you could just go about what you needed to do whenever you wanted, right? Unfortunately, as we know, that is not the case, and you need to firstly have a clear concept of what time is in order to even attempt to manage it.

This is not about being able to tell the time – though that certainly helps – it is more about knowing what time you have available, and then how you can best manage it.

What does time management mean for you as a student?

Time management is about knowing what you need to do (which is where organisation comes into it – more on that in the upcoming chapters), and then knowing what time you have available to complete the task/s or activities.

Although it is a fact that time management isn't fully developed until the age of 25, that doesn't mean you can't learn to manage it much earlier. It is a valuable skill that can certainly be learned, but it does require effort over time for you to do so effectively. For some people it does come more naturally than it does for others, but each and every one of us has the ability to change our behaviours and put strategies into practice to help us with our time.

Time management can help you, as a student, to do everyday things like:

- Manage what you need to on a daily basis
- Get yourself ready
- Get to school on time
- Manage and attend classes
- Undertake afterschool activities
- Get homework done
- Complete assignments
- Prepare for assessment tasks
- Study for tests and exams

Time management is something that, as a student, you want on your side.

How to use time

Once you establish what time you actually have, it is then very much about having the ability to use your time effectively and productively.

When a student doesn't use their time wisely, life can easily feel less balanced, and you can become stressed and/or overwhelmed. We all want to avoid these feelings where possible as it usually only makes tasks even more challenging and difficult to complete.

As a student, the most wasted time of your day is often from after school to dinnertime. Even if you know what time you have available, it is important for you to also know how long a task is going to take (more on that in Chapter 2).

To get time management working for you, it is about having a plan and then having the ability to take action. Sounds rather simple, right? Unfortunately, it is often not that easy and there are many things that can get in our way. We will take a look at some of these throughout this book.

Definition of time management

The official definitions of time management that I tend to use when working with students are:

- The ability to use one's time effectively or productively
- Making the most of the time available to accomplish what needs to get done
- Planning and organising one's time every day to focus on tasks that need to be completed

In addition to the above, it is also important to try to have balance, though this might not always be possible every single day.

Another way to explain this, is that you can look at time management in two parts:

1. Having a plan, knowing your approach and altering it if necessary
2. Executing the plan in a timely and productive manner

Planning ahead links closely to time management, and it is important for students to ensure there are no unnecessary surprises. How often have you remembered the night before, or on the actual day, that you have work due or a test? It isn't a nice feeling when you haven't had time to prepare or complete the work, and something as students we want to try and avoid happening.

In the next chapter, we look in more detail at how you can actually manage time.

CHAPTER 2

Managing time

Now that you have a clear understanding of what time management means, how does one go about managing it?

Managing time can relate to all of the following aspects of your life: daily, weekly, fortnightly, monthly and even shorter or longer timeframes.

In order to manage time and tasks, believe it or not, you need to be able to see time in the first place. What does this actually mean? There are five key concepts which I feel necessary to explain to increase your understanding.

1. Now vs not now

It is natural for students, particularly in secondary school, to pretty much live in the 'now' versus the 'not now'. To understand what I mean by this, I want to firstly explore the term 'executive functions', which basically help us to get stuff done.

Every human being has executive functions which assist with organisation, planning, prioritising, focus and motivation as well as managing time. For some of us, we probably don't even really think about these, whereas for others, they can have more challenges in some or all of these areas (check out Chapter 12 for more ideas if this is you).

When it comes to time, it is important to understand the actual difference between the 'now' and the 'not now':

> The **'now'** is very much being aware of the present moment; it is pretty much just focusing on the here and now.

> The **'not now'** is more about what is coming up in the future – this could be what might be coming up in a short period of time or later on the same day, tomorrow, next week or even longer into one's future.

Now that you understand both of the above, you can probably work out which applies more specifically to you – or are you a mix of both the 'now' and the 'not now'? There is no right or wrong answer to this question. What *is* important is that you need to be aware of these concepts, as both can assist you when it comes to getting things done for both school and in other areas of your life.

Another thing to note is that it can sometimes be hard for students to move from the 'now' to the 'not now'. Sometimes we can get caught up in what we are currently doing and then put off or not do what needs to be done.

One of the key challenges for students with these two concepts is that they don't always see into the future, which can be the next day or further on in time. For example, you might not see what is coming up, i.e. that maths test next week or an assignment that's due in 10 days' time. This can make it difficult and often you don't prepare enough for the test or rush to complete work at the last minute. As a result, this can impact on how you feel, and many students start to feel overwhelmed or stressed. Naturally, we want to avoid these feelings as no one likes to experience these.

2. Concept of time

Another key aspect when it comes to managing one's time is understanding that time always has a beginning, middle and an end. As an example, you might be given a task today to complete and hand in two weeks from now. Therefore, today is the beginning of the time to begin that task; the end is the due date; and the time in between is the middle. Pretty much all of the things we do at school and in other areas of our lives involve us following this concept.

Growing up, you have no doubt learnt to tell the time and for many of us it was most likely by using an analogue clock. One benefit of analogue clocks is that they clearly show us that time has a beginning, a middle and an end. We have the ability to see time actually ticking or passing by through these stages.

Think about this compared to digital technology which surrounds us today. If you look at the time on your phone or your computer, all you see is the current time and not the ability to see the time go by. Digital technology has in some ways both simplified and made our lives more complicated at the same time. By not seeing time in the way described on the previous page with analogue clocks, we can struggle to manage it effectively and often run out of time to do what we need to. As a student, what you need to do is often homework, an assignment or preparing for an assessment. How often have you found yourself madly doing this at the last minute, feeling pressured?

3. Seeing time

To ensure we are managing time effectively, it is important for students to see time and to create an awareness of the future. This means you know not only what you need to do today, but also what is coming up in the future that needs dealing with. One of the best ways to do this is to get into the habit of regularly looking ahead. I suggest you do this by seeing, at a minimum, what is coming up ahead in the next few days and up to a week.

Seeing ahead allows you to not only be aware of what is coming up, but to also start taking action and planning what you need to get done in the lead-up, rather than at the last minute. Now, think about upcoming homework, assignments or assessments. By actually seeing what it is that's coming up and by knowing when it is due, you are taking a key step in creating a future awareness.

My very first student was a girl in Year 9 who was extremely busy as she was a top athlete in her sport, which she juggled with the academic demands of school. When we started working together, she was feeling very overwhelmed about how she was going to manage all that she needed to do. The first step was for her to actually see what time she had alongside all of the activities in her life, so we plotted it out. Up to that point, she really had no idea of the amount of time she was actually using. Once she could see what time she had available, she realised that she in fact had plenty of time for her sporting activities, managing her schoolwork and having balance with time to do things she enjoyed.

Do you know where your time goes and what time you might have available? If you are not very sure, then it can be useful to plot this out. Remember, in order to manage time, you need to see it first!

To help us further with seeing time, we need to use planning tools, which you can read more about in Chapter 5.

4. The three Ws

Another important concept to help you is to know what I refer to as the three Ws: What, When and Where.

This links into seeing time as mentioned in concept 3, and in order for students to manage their time, it is essential to know:

- **What** – what you need to do or what you have on; knowing what the task involves and the steps you are likely to have to take. It can also include what you need to complete the task as well, i.e. resources – do you need books, worksheets, pencils, a certain program or equipment?

- **When** – when you need to be somewhere. Does it have a start and finish time, etc? Being punctual and ready to go is important, i.e. you start school at 9am or you need to be at your afterschool job which starts at 4pm. This doesn't mean arriving exactly at that time, but rather being there ahead of the actual start time and being ready and prepared.

- **Where** – where will this take place? Do you need to factor in time before or after? Do you need time to get to where you need to be, i.e. travel time?

I encourage you to always keep the three Ws in mind when it comes to managing and organising your time at secondary school as it will be helpful over and over again.

5. Estimating and using time

Following on from knowing what you have to do, the next concept to understand and put into practice is being able to estimate how long a task or something you need to do is likely to take. Have a think for a moment... Have you had an experience similar to this: you were given a task and thought it would only take a certain amount of time, however, when you got into it, you realised there was more to it, and you didn't have enough time to complete it before it was due. If this has happened to you, it is certainly not a nice feeling to have, is it?

The ability to estimate time is such an important skill to understand and continue to develop in order to assist you with your schoolwork and tasks. The main aspect of this is to ensure that you are not underestimating the time needed for tasks and then run out of time when things come up or when you have a heavy workload to manage all of these things at once.

If this is something you struggle with, then you can take steps to change and ensure you have enough time to accomplish your tasks. Here are a couple of tips and strategies to consider putting into practice:

- Ask your teacher for an indication of how long they expect a task you are assigned will take. This can then be used as a guide, i.e. you have an essay to write, and the teacher said it should take about an hour; some students might complete it in less than that and for others it might take a bit longer.
- Begin making estimates yourself for each of your homework or assignment tasks – it doesn't matter if they are not accurate initially. Over time, by doing this regularly you will get a better handle on how long something will take.

Don't you think it will be much easier for you to manage your time more effectively now that you know all of the above concepts? If you think 'yes', then what are you waiting for? You can start today by putting these into practice or getting better at approaching them. Using and managing your time more wisely will allow you more time for the things you enjoy and want to be doing.

CHAPTER 3

What does it mean to be organised?

Now that you know what time management is, the next key element is to know what organisation means and how this, too, can impact you both at school and in other areas of your life.

Organisation is different for each of us, and to some it comes more naturally than it does for others. It is an important tool that can assist us, and I am sure you can probably think of times when it helped you, and also times when you weren't organised and it had an impact on you.

What does organisation mean?

One of the usual definitions that I give to students is that it means the action of organising something. As a student, there are many things that you need to organise (see more on this below).

When it comes to organisation, there is no right or wrong way to do something – it is about finding what works best for you, i.e. how your friend does it might not best suit you, and vice versa.

For example, if I asked you to organise a pencil case you might like to organise it by colours. Someone else will organise it by putting pens, pencils and other items into piles. Another person could organise it differently again. You need to find your own organisational strategies in order for them to help you at school and in other areas of your life.

Organisation helps us to:

- Establish what we want to do
- Know where to begin a task
- Understand the sequence in which to carry out a task (what is needed, i.e. equipment)
- Problem-solve in the event of a challenge or roadblock
- Have the ability to persist with a task to completion (and in an appropriate timeframe when it comes to schoolwork, i.e. meeting deadlines)

For the majority of us, it is important for our belongings to all have a place or be neat/tidy so that we can easily find and access them when we need to. How often have you wasted time not being able to find something quickly? This is why it is useful for our belongings to have 'a home', and for us to know where they are kept, which ultimately saves us time when we need to get something at another point in time.

What do you need to organise?

When I ask students this question, they usually include most of the below:

- First and foremost yourself – knowing the three Ws: What, When and Where, mentioned in Chapter 2, i.e. what books you need to have, when you need to be in class (what time) and what room the class is in (where)
- Tubs/lockers – so you can find what you need easily
- Bags – so they are not like a black hole and hard to find your belongings
- Books – these include your notebooks and textbooks
- Notes and handouts – where you take your notes (written or electronically), where you store them and also keeping worksheets/booklets
- Where to find the necessary details of work you need to complete
- Where to do your homework, study or revision – one or several places
- Managing homework, assignments and assessment tasks
- Having the necessary resources you need to complete your work
- Completing homework and tasks and ensuring they are handed in on time
- Being prepared for tests, assessments and exams

Many of the components on the previous page apply to both how you manage things at school and at home as well. Ultimately, organisation helps us with our time; when we are not organised, or have a particular routine to follow, then a lot of time can be wasted.

Your bedroom and desk space, when messy and unorganised, can cause you stress and can take you away from the key task at hand as you might feel the need to clean up and sort out your space first. If these spaces are not tended to on a regular basis, they can take away a lot of time.

CHAPTER 4

What role does organisation play?

Further to the previous chapter, there are some other important aspects to understand when it comes to organisation for students.

Knowing what one needs to do

The very first step at school, as mentioned in Chapter 2, is being able to see time and tasks. This relates to ensuring you record key information every day in your classes. More specifically, this means including the details of tasks and due dates. (You can read more about using a planning tool in Chapter 5.)

If you are not understanding or are missing something about assigned tasks, then it is important to ask your teacher for further details (see Chapter 10 for more on how you might do this).

The other part of this puzzle that needs completing is knowing where to find further information and then regularly having a system or process to help find it. This involves navigating and checking online portals or relevant apps you might use for a particular subject to ensure you can also find further details about tasks in relation to the information you are learning.

Starting the year with good intentions

Usually students have the desire to want to do as well at school as they possibly can. They often start a new school year or term with enthusiasm and usually put in the necessary effort and focus. Sound familiar so far?

Most students have various intentions that often include things like:

- To be more organised than before
- To keep papers and lockers tidy
- To be better at managing time and tasks
- To keep up with, and on top of, work
- To submit everything on time
- To get good results

So, what happens to alter this?

Dealing with dips in the road

At some point, and for many different reasons, students often get about four to six weeks in and the intentions they have start to change. This change is usually first reflected in students not achieving the marks they usually get or are capable of getting. Or it can be related to incomplete homework, which was rushed and done at the last minute, and even handed in late.

It can also be at this time when students experience and start to demonstrate any number of the following:

- Feeling a lack of motivation
- Getting more easily distracted
- Finding themselves procrastinating
- Struggling to self-start
- Having difficulty with focusing and concentration
- Struggling with effort
- Becoming more unorganised
- Struggling to have a realistic idea of the time and effort needed to complete tasks

As a result of the above, it is not uncommon to see a student also struggle more with overwhelm, stress and anxiety at this time.

Another way to describe 'the dip' is that it is like a road that goes up and down with a lot of dips along the way. For some students, the dips will be larger than for others.

For some students, it can be almost complete avoidance, and for others, the 'swimming back upstream' starts where they are keen to get back on top, but can often seem to feel they are always playing catch-up.

So, what can you do if you feel this happens to you?

The most important step is to initially recognise 'the dip' so that action can be taken to turn things around. For some students it can be caught in time so that, with a few changes made, they can get back on track relatively easily.

However, for others, it can be more of a challenge. It often requires quite a bit of time and perseverance from the student in particular. It can also require small steps to be made rather than to expect changes to be sorted in one go.

In order to have any success in attempting to fix 'the dip', you will need to:

- Have the right skills and strategies to change your mindset and deal with any resistance you might feel
- Know what the right systems are and put these into place
- Build back or create new habits and routines
- Seek practical strategies that will work for you

In my experience it is worth talking to either a teacher, parent or older sibling to discuss what can be done. Try and get on to this early as, unfortunately, the longer it goes on, the harder it can be to get back on track.

Having routines and creating habits

Many students struggle to create regular routines and habits. Most people do function better when these are in place, even though it might not be something students are willing to admit to themselves or even to their families.

Routines and habits provide consistency and will help you to manage everything you need to in your day and help you to stay on top much easier than if you don't have them in place.

Let's take a moment so you can have a think about all the things you have in your day; this might include:

- School
- Afterschool activities like sport, training, going to the gym
- A part-time job
- Chores at home

You get the gist.

Naturally, all students differ as to what they might have, and even the days of the week can differ, too – some of you will have a lot to do and others will have very little on different days.

In your regular daily routine you also need to include:

- Having regular sleep
- Keeping on top of personal hygiene
- Having some downtime

The important thing to remember is that while you have a routine, it doesn't have to be completely strict so that you can't alter it or do anything else. The key is to aim to have a regular routine to make what you need to manage easier and ensure you get everything done that you need to in your day, including completing schoolwork.

Spend some time thinking about your morning and afterschool/evening routine that you have now. What could you do to make it better for you? A handy tip for the morning could be to work backwards from the time school starts and think about what you need to fit into your morning, i.e. having a shower, eating breakfast, walking the dog, and then ensure you are waking up in time to fit everything in.

Many students can struggle to get up in the mornings, so it is important to ensure that as part of your afternoon/evening routine you are getting to bed at a reasonable time to get enough sleep. It is recommended that teenagers should be getting a minimum of eight to 10 hours sleep every night. Are you getting this on a regular basis? If not, then you might like to give some thought to your evening routine, and how you might be able to ensure you get to bed a bit earlier. Even as little as 15 to 30 minutes more can make a difference.

Finally, having regular routines in place can help you to keep stress and anxiety at bay as well as succeed better at school.

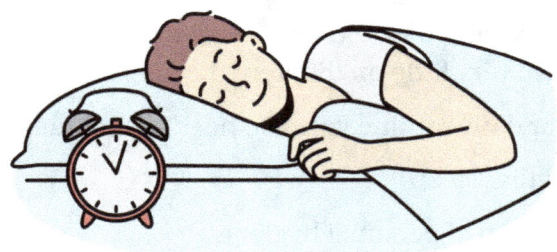

Prepare ahead of time

One such routine or habit is to prepare the night before, particularly if you are not a morning person. Look at the upcoming day and get out what you will need for it and put it into your bag ready, i.e. have you got PE tomorrow? You might even like to ensure you have all your uniform out so you don't have to go looking for that pair of socks in the morning or something else that can take time.

It can also be useful to get into the habit of looking ahead further than just the next day. What I often suggest to students is, say, on a Sunday night, look at the upcoming week and put some time into planning ahead for everything you might have coming up. Even just being aware of what is likely to be happening can make things easier for you to manage. (You can read more about the importance of planning in Chapter 6.)

Regular maintenance is key

The maintenance aspect is more key than the organisation itself and is often where things can fall over. I regularly tell students that getting organised is the easy part and maintenance is the hard part. So, what do I mean by that?

Often we can spend time getting ourselves organised, but then don't follow through with the same pattern or behaviour on a regular basis. Let me use the example of cleaning up your bedroom. Over a few weeks you have found your room has piles of clothes (both clean and dirty) on the floor; there are also empty food wrappers, dirty glasses or plates, piles of worksheets and books on your desk and all over the place... You might spend an hour putting everything away in its place and making it organised again. If you don't then regularly spend time putting things away, it is most likely you will find yourself back in the same situation again very soon.

A good way to approach this might be for you to once a week set a regular time to sort and put stuff away so that you will then only be dealing with a week's worth of stuff rather than months. It will also be much quicker to do this routinely than having to find a big chunk of time to do it periodically.

Another area that students sometimes struggle with is the organisation of papers, booklets, worksheets, notes and files. Best practice is to have a system in place for keeping relevant materials by subject rather than in one pile or scrunched up in one's locker. If these do get a bit unorganised from time to time, make a habit of sorting them into the relevant folder or workbook to make it easier to find and refer to later. The challenge here is that students often don't think they will need these materials again, however, they can be quite useful when preparing for assessments or exams at a later time.

One suggestion is to have small plastic folders for each subject at home in a book box, and then when you are finished with materials, to put them in the relevant folder. That way, you have them on hand for when you might need them, and you won't have to spend time looking for them or sorting through piles of information.

Remember, nowadays it is also important to have a system for electronic files in order for information to be found quickly when needed. A key point to note is to ensure that anything kept online is backed up so that should something happen to your device, you won't lose important material.

CHAPTER 5

How planning tools can help

With more information for students being posted online in school portals, students often believe they don't need to use planning tools. This is WRONG – you do!

It is common to hear students complain about having to write or note down tasks, assignments or tests in their own planning tool as often it is noted on the school portal or in another app the teacher might be using. I get it – I know you don't want to do it, but you SHOULD. I am sure you have had teachers that haven't always put the necessary information up on the school portal.

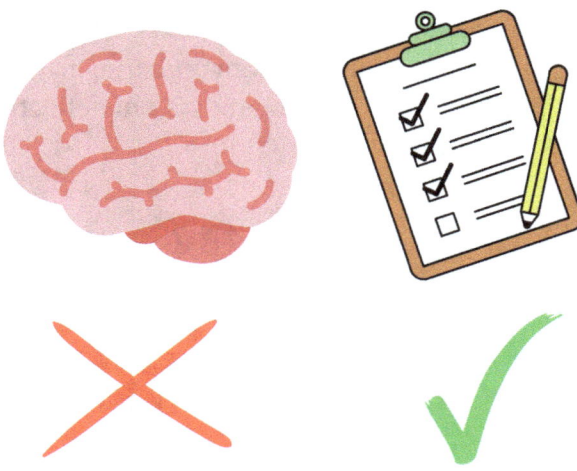

A planning tool is not just useful for noting necessary information – it is so much more than that and should be seen as an extension of your brain. A student's brain is not made to remember all the tasks they need to do – something will get forgotten sooner or later. A student's short-term, or working, memory only holds two to four bits of information at a time. Trying to remember work that needs completing as well as your learning and the task at hand all increases the mental load and isn't the most effective strategy in the longer term.

In Chapter 2, you learned that in order to manage time you need to make it visible. If you can't see something, then it can be like it doesn't actually exist. Remember, too, that deadlines can have a habit of creeping up and can create unnecessary stress and overwhelm if not managed effectively. Many successful students will often tell you it isn't just about knowing the subject content, but more importantly, it's the tools they have used to help them be organised and manage their time which have led to their success.

Often younger students will say they don't really have a lot to remember and manage. They also regularly say they can just use their head to do so. If this is you, then my advice is to start creating good habits around using a planning tool early to set yourself up for when you do get really busy and have many more tasks to manage.

A planning tool gives you structure to get work done more efficiently and effectively, as well as more freedom and time to do other things. Please note, though, that a planning tool is only effective if you are willing to work with, and actually use, it.

Finding the right tool/s

There was a time when all that students used was a paper diary for school; however, nowadays, there are so many more options available. All different planning tools have both pros and cons, and it is very much about finding the right tool/s that suit you and are going to work for you. It might take a bit of trial and error and giving a few options a go before you settle on the one that's right for you.

Here are my top suggestions:

- Paper planner/diary – ideally a week to a page view
- Electronic calendars – Google Calendar, iCalendar
- Sticky notes on the desktop
- Paper wall or desk calendar
- Reusable wall planners – ideally, monthly or term focused to see ahead of time as weekly isn't as helpful
- Apps – Notion, Todoist, Microsoft To Do, myHomework, MyStudyLife, Big Day, Event Countdown, Exam Countdown, Mindlist, Structured (otherwise Google 'planning apps' for current options)
- ClickUp
- School Portal or school-created apps – sometimes there are options to also track work on a school system by putting in and including your own information/details

Some students also like to use a mixture of options like sticky notes in class and then putting the details on a wall planner at home.

How to use planning tools

Once you have settled on a planning tool to use, the next step is to work out how you should use it.

Often this is where students fall over as they are not always sure how to use it effectively in order for it to work for them.

There are a minimum of five key things that you will need to include:

1. Take note of the task or assignment on the day you get it and include the due date.//
2. Input the task on the due date and make it stand out so that it is really clear to see. It is important that when you input the work you don't just write the subject, topic or words like 'study' or 'revision'. It needs to be specific and have the necessary detail, i.e. maths questions – Chapter 8 A to H. By noting down the detail, you are more likely to follow through with the task.

3. Find and allocate time to work on the task between now and when it is due, and note this down in the planning tool. Some tasks need to be planned out, so why not use the planner to help with this? Determine the specific steps and break them down, then list them on the days that you can work on them.

4. Include all other activities, i.e. sport, hobbies, family events, etc. Including these allows you to clearly see when you can actually find time to do the work (as per point 3 above).

5. At the end of every week, go through the week that has passed and if any tasks have not been completed, reallocate them and find time to do them in the week ahead.

At the end of the day, using a planning tool really does make life so much easier. As a student, why wouldn't you want to be more effective and efficient with your time so that you then have more freedom and time for other activities you enjoy? Why not just give it a go and see? What have you got to lose?

CHAPTER 6

The importance of planning

Planning goes hand in hand with organisation and ultimately links quite closely to time management, too. As already mentioned, preparing ahead of time is a valuable approach to getting into the habit of doing, and can ultimately assist you to save potential time as well. Ideally, you want to be aware of what is coming up so there are no surprises. Your workload also needs to be front of mind at all times as you don't want to forget anything. Regular habits around planning will help you.

Without a plan it is very easy to get stressed, feel overwhelmed and in general feel like you are always playing catch-up. I am sure you can probably relate to a time when you got behind and how this might have made you feel. In most experiences, when a student struggles to stay on top of their workload, it can be challenging trying to catch up and feel on top again.

So, if you haven't already done so, I suggest that you get into the habit of planning out what you need to do – it can also help you have better balance in your life. Of course, there will be times when you are likely to be busier than others, and planning for this in advance where you can, will certainly be useful to you.

Here are some practical planning strategies for you to consider…

Preparing a schedule

In Chapter 5, we addressed the importance of using a planning tool. What is being highlighted here is more about putting together your own weekly or monthly schedule and using that, along with your planning tool, to work out what you can do and when, around any activities or events you might have on. Remember, in order to manage time, you need to 'see' time. By having a schedule and reviewing on a regular basis what you have on will help you to keep up and stay on top.

Another key time when planning ahead and putting together a schedule can help students is in the lead-up to exams. If you plan ahead to exams, you can ensure you have enough time to revise and prepare. In an ideal world, the minimum timeframe for you to do this is, for younger students, three weeks prior, and more senior students, about six weeks.

This book doesn't focus solely on study skills; however, very briefly, an exam plan should include what you are going to study and when – be specific with tasks and ensure an even amount of time is approximately spread across preparing for all subjects.

One final point: when it comes to exam planning, please don't leave it until exams are nearly upon you to prepare. It is equally important to be putting strategies into place on a regular basis throughout the year in terms of learning and consolidating your knowledge.

Being realistic

Knowing what time you have available, by looking ahead and planning this out along with knowing how long a task is likely to take (refer to Chapter 2 for more details on this), will allow you to set realistic timeframes to complete tasks.

Being realistic also helps you to stay motivated, focused and ultimately manage your time more effectively and to feel more in control. It is also much less stressful, too!

One strategy that might be helpful is, once you have estimated how long you think you will need, allow another one to one and a half times more time on top. Remember, it is usually better to overestimate, ensuring you have enough time, rather than to underestimate and not have enough time.

Completing assignments or longer-term tasks

When you find yourself having assignments or longer-term tasks to work on – including maybe several tasks at the same time across your subjects – it can be a bit of a challenge to work out how you are going to manage. This is usually where a student can struggle and start feeling overwhelmed.

When you get some key dates for tasks, it can then be useful right at the start to work out your approach to how you are going to tackle each task. For instance, work backwards from the due date and ensure you allocate enough time to do what you need to, i.e. in your planning tool, note down the date on which the task must be completed, then add a date for the draft, then a date for the near final, allowing a few extra days to review before handing it in. This is where planning ahead can certainly help!

Breaking tasks down

Another strategy of planning is knowing how to break tasks down to ultimately make the process easier for you and assist with potential overwhelm and stress.

How often have you had a task in the past that when you have looked at it you got the feeling there was just too much to do? What did you do then? Usually most students will put it down and say to themselves that they will deal with it later. This is an all too familiar experience for students and is procrastination 101 occurring right there.

Next time you get a larger task or start to have a feeling like the one described above, I suggest you break down the task into smaller tasks immediately. By breaking tasks down, you create chunks of work which are then much easier and more manageable for you to make a start on or find the time to complete.

One such method to break down tasks can be the Traffic Light Method, whereby you get the three colours of a traffic light and highlight how you relate to each task or step in the process.

It works like this:

- Red = those things you don't know how to do or will need help with.
- Orange or yellow = things you are not entirely sure about but could probably work out or make a start on.
- Green = things you can do easily.

By adopting this strategy, you can then work out your approach to the overall project and chip away at it bit by bit.

Being prepared for things to get in the way

While planning is important, you also need to allow for life being unpredictable sometimes. As you probably already know, this can happen at any time despite having the best laid-out plans or intentions. Having the ability to be flexible and adaptable are also useful skills for you to develop for when this occurs. Should something interrupt your plans, then take action and make changes by adjusting your approach with a new plan.

In any plan you also need to be aware of other challenges that can get in your way, like procrastination and distractions (see Chapter 8 for more on these).

CHAPTER 7

Being effective and productive

In an ideal world, we would all be effective and productive with our time. However, this isn't always the case. In this chapter, you will find some suggestions to consider putting in place to help you use your time as efficiently as you can.

By being more effective, you are likely to then have more time to spend on other things that you like doing outside of being a student and completing schoolwork. Remember, it is all about having a balance between school and other activities.

Setting goals

Having goals can help with being motivated and using one's time effectively. Goals are basically like setting yourself a roadmap to where you want to go. It can be challenging to use time well if you don't know what to do with it.

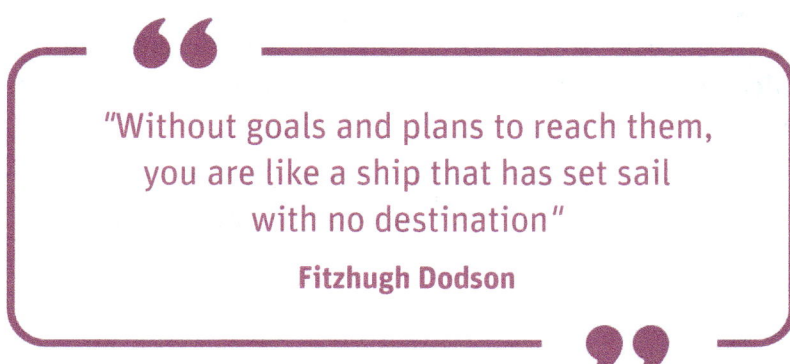

"Without goals and plans to reach them, you are like a ship that has set sail with no destination"

Fitzhugh Dodson

Learning how to set and achieve goals is a life skill that can be useful during your secondary school journey and into the future.

One framework that can help you in setting goals is the SMART goals framework. This can be used to set both academic and personal goals into your day (short term) or for something in the longer term. It is relatively easy to understand and will assist you to develop your own goals and help you plan towards reaching them.

SMART goals framework

S = specific: Define your goal in detail – what is it you want to achieve?

M = measurable: Decide how you will measure it so you can easily see if you achieve it or not.

A = attainable/achievable: Set realistic goals that challenge you but are achievable. Also have a specific timeframe in mind.

R = realistic, relevant and results focused: Your goals should include only those things that you can do and follow through with.

T = timely and trackable: Set clear deadlines and monitor your progress.

An example of a short-term goal might be to aim to complete your homework straight after school each day to enable you to then have the rest of the evening to relax; or it might be to aim to go to the gym three times a week. A long-term goal might be to improve your results in English from a C to a B; make the first football team; or get a particular ATAR result (or your relevant final mark in your location) in Year 12.

If you do decide to set some goals in place, then remember that you will need to dedicate time towards achieving them as they won't be accomplished by themselves.

Create a time log

It could be useful for you to create your own time log to track how you are actually using your time. You could do this for a day, a couple of days or even a week. It might be a real eye-opener to see where your time goes, and assist you to ascertain whether you are being effective or ineffective.

You could start it from the moment you get home from school till when you go to bed, or from the time you sit down to do your schoolwork till when you finish completing it. Note down the entire time, including when you have a break, get distracted, let your mind wander, etc.

It can also be very useful for you to be able to see a clock when completing schoolwork so that you can be aware of the time and how long something may be taking you.

Once you gain a sense of what you are doing with your time, and become more aware of how you spend it, then you can begin to work towards minimising wasting time and being more effective.

Using time wisely at school

Attending class every day is a given for students. However, students are not always as focused and effective with their time in the classroom as they could be. Some days can seem tougher and longer than others and at times it can be challenging to maintain focus, not get distracted or zone out.

Classes are primarily conducted so that students can gain an understanding of the subject content and have the opportunity to ask questions. Sometimes there is even time available to complete tasks to consolidate the learning.

The more you can pay attention, listen and complete work in class, the more productive you are ultimately going to be. When you don't do this, you are more likely to have to spend additional time outside of class relearning or completing the work. By adopting the approach of 'I'll do it later' is only potentially setting you up to struggle later on.

It really is a no-brainer then for you to use class time rather than your own time on top of the class time to complete work. Naturally, not all work will get completed in class, and additional homework can still be handed out, but using class time means there will be less of your own time that you will have to use later.

Prioritising is key

Many students like to begin working on something they enjoy or find easier, and this can be helpful in order to make a start. However, what is not helpful is when students do all the work they enjoy or find easier and leave the tasks they don't like or find harder until the end. If this sounds like you, you might find that you struggle to find the motivation to continue working on tasks, and you begin to procrastinate and be put off by the tasks. It can therefore be useful at the beginning to mix the work up by starting with something you like followed by something you like less, and so on.

One such approach that might help is for you to put together a quick plan as soon as you get home from school with what you need to get done that night. This should ideally be done before taking a break and moving completely out of school mode. You can create the plan on a piece of paper or a whiteboard; include a list of tasks, an estimation of how long each task will take, and then a priority list for completing tasks. Having a plan such as this will help to keep you focused, get tasks done and procrastinate less.

> 1. Review today's notes (15 minutes)
> 2. Biology assignment (1 hour)
> 4. English essay (45 minutes)
> 3. Maths questions (30 minutes)

It's a good idea to try different approaches to work out which works best for you. And remember, it doesn't have to be rigid; you can alter and adopt different approaches at different times, too. Sometimes having different options or processes to follow can provide variety – and it's also less boring that way!

Knowing how to get started

Students usually know what they need to do, but it is often the action of getting started that can be the struggle. Sometimes it is due to:

- Having a lot of work to do
- Looking at the overall amount of time that it will likely take to get the work done
- Not wanting to even do the work in the first place

Do any of these sound like you?

When all or some of the above occurs, students can begin to feel stressed or overwhelmed. Rather than letting yourself start to feel this way, it can be helpful to just focus on making a start, for even just two to five minutes, or by completing one question of the 10 that you need to do. This can help some students and often gets them into the groove to keep going. Others might have to keep doing it in this way, bit by bit or one step at a time, which is OK, too.

Avoid multitasking

Many of us believe that we can do multiple things at the same time. Students are more often tempted to do this when they get busy and have a bit they need to accomplish.

Let me first explain multitasking and how it links to what you might be doing. It can include:

- Completing two or more tasks at the same time (including listening to music)
- Moving back and forth between tasks (i.e. focusing on your worksheet and then switching to social media)
- Doing a number of tasks quickly back to back (answering a question, reading notes from another subject and then revising notes)

While you might think you can do this, it is usually not the best approach to take and students can often find themselves being inefficient and achieving very little.

Remember, the ultimate goal in completing homework or doing some study/revision is to consolidate one's knowledge. By trying to multitask, what is actually happening is that you are dividing your attention to multiple things at the same time and, therefore, while you might feel you are learning what you need to, it is unlikely that is actually what is going on in your brain. It gets tired much faster, too, so the information is less likely to be making its way to the parts of the brain where it needs to be in order for you to recall it later on. In other words, it can impair your memory.

Task switching also makes time less productive and it can actually take longer to complete work. On top of this, you are more likely to start making mistakes.

Therefore, it is to your benefit to focus on one task at a time – that way, you will be more productive, too.

Other helpful tools

Put together checklists to help you with what you are wanting to achieve. For example, have a checklist that reminds you of:

- What you need to do each afternoon when you get home from school
- The different approaches or steps you can be doing with your homework, study or revision
- Listing the things you need to do each morning before you go to school

Remember that teachers often provide rubrics, checklists, outlines or revision lists – make sure you use and refer to these, as they are there to assist you to know what you need to do. It regularly amazes me as to how little some students use these tools which have been provided to them. Why wouldn't you use them when they often lay everything out very clearly and will help to make everything easier for you to get the result you want?

One important final point to highlight is that being productive isn't about studying for longer periods of time. It is more about being effective and efficient with the time that you have.

By incorporating some of the above suggestions into your routine, you will be able to improve the quality of what you do, reduce overwhelm and stress, and ultimately achieve better academic results at school. As I regularly say, it is about studying smarter, not harder. Don't you think that is something you, too, would like to do?

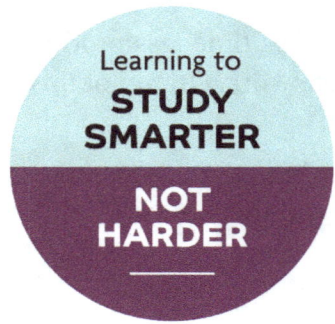

CHAPTER 8

Managing procrastination and distractions

At the end of the day, it is key to ensure you get your work done, and to do this, you need to know how to overcome procrastination and to manage distractions.

What is procrastination?

Procrastination is something that can rob you of your time and affect your ability to complete the required work to the best of your ability. It is estimated that more than 90% of students procrastinate and put off schoolwork until tomorrow when they should start today – does this sound like something you do?

Some reasons why students procrastinate include:

- Not knowing where to start
- Thinking you have more time than you do
- Not having an understanding of what needs to be completed
- Having no set homework or study routine
- Getting distracted (more on that over the page)
- Fear of failing
- Perfectionism – trying to get something done perfectly or in a certain way

What are distractions?

A distraction is something that interferes with your work as a student and prevents you from concentrating on your learning in class or on completing a set task.

Distractions have the ability, like procrastination, to:

- Rob you of the time you have available to complete work or study
- Take away your focus and then, unfortunately, the quality of your work can suffer
- Increase your feelings of stress, overwhelm and levels of anxiety

Having focus is vital and, as a student, you need to be aware that by allowing distractions to occur, you are potentially forcing your brain to spend time and effort loading and reloading over and over again the context of what you are doing. This often occurs without you even realising it is happening!

You might believe that it is possible to multitask, however, as explained in the previous chapter, you often get very little done and can even feel tired in the process. What you do is burn all your energy switching your focus and attention rather than actually making any progress with what you need to achieve or complete.

Another downside to getting distracted is that very little information from what you are working on finds its way into your long-term memory (which is where you need it to be in order to recall and achieve in tests and exams).

How to manage procrastination and distractions

In order to do something about procrastination and distractions, you need to:

- Know yourself
- Be aware of when they are occurring
- Be able to identify how they affect you
- The behaviours/habits that cause them or bring them on

Most students have a sincere desire to complete their homework/assignments or revision, however, they often come unstuck. In an ideal world, every time you sit down to complete your schoolwork, you would just be able to do it without any issues.

Unfortunately, it isn't an ideal world and things can get in the way of our desire to get work done. But equipped with the right tools you can avoid, delay or swerve around procrastination and manage any distractions.

Here are four essential gears that can help

One way to describe what you need is something like gears that all need to work together to operate just like they do for a machine. As a student, you need to have four gears in place to connect your desire to get your work done with actually completing it. Here are the four gears:

1. **The first gear represents having the right TOOLS** – this means using a planner, calendar, diary and reminders (as discussed in Chapter 5), to ensure that time becomes visible to you. Other tools might include quizzable study tools, office supplies, textbooks, etc.

   Having tools alone, though, is usually not enough, and you need another tool that helps you to follow through.

2. **The second gear represents having the right ROUTINES** – this gear is important and helps you to get started on your homework/assignments/revision. Having the right routines like a clear homework plan, breaking tasks down (mentioned in Chapter 6 and there's more information coming on this) or working in blocks of time like 20 minutes on and five minutes off, using a timer or setting reminders to prompt you into action, can all help you to make a start.

   Sometimes with the right tools and routines you can actually get moving on the work you need to complete, however, to make it happen more easily and with more flow, there are still two more gears needed.

3. **The third gear represents having the right TEAM** – this gear involves using people to help you to follow through. As a student, sometimes it is easy to think you have to tackle everything by yourself when you actually don't. As human beings, we usually tend to work better when we have others around. It is great to use other people to make you accountable for what you need to do. Sometimes just the presence of others can be enough – working with a friend, or using a parent to help

or getting them to check in with you from time to time to see you are on task.

We now have the right tools, routines and team and are getting closer, but are still not getting our homework or tasks completed. This leads us to the final gear.

4. **The fourth gear represents SELF-TALK** – the final tool for students to avoid procrastinating is self-talk, which are the things you tell yourself about your work. How often do you tell yourself something like, 'I can do this tomorrow as there is still plenty of time'? This is so common, and you need to be aware of your thoughts that might be getting in your way of starting and finishing your work, so you can transform and reframe these to allow you to, firstly, make a start and, secondly, get your work done.

Now that you have all four gears in place, they can each link to 1) the desire to get your homework or assignments done, and 2) the actual element that represents the homework or assignments themselves.

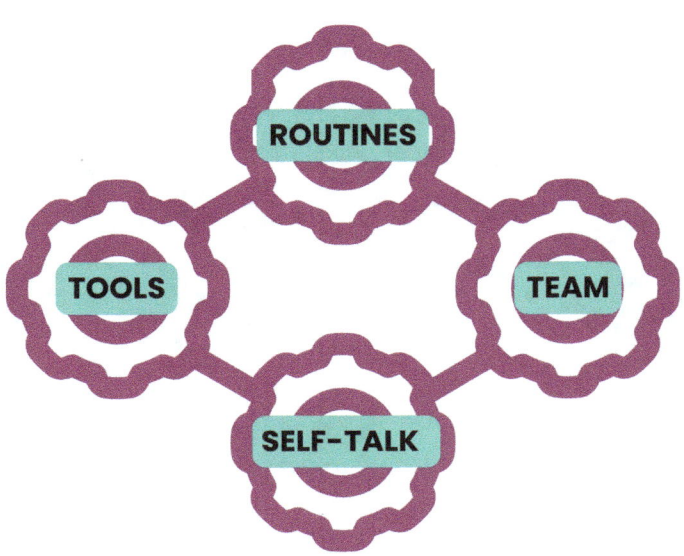

If you are finding yourself having trouble getting your work done, then use the four gears as a checklist to see what is or isn't working for you at a specific time. Being aware of these can help you to take action and do something about it!

Removing distractions

It is important that you either remove the distractions that are likely to tempt you – i.e. your mobile phone, an app on your device or something else – or you move to a place where there are no distractions so that you can concentrate on completing your work.

Breaking tasks down

Often students look at what they need to achieve and focus on the end result. For example, you might have an essay to write and all you are thinking is that it is going to take hours. Thinking in this way can be unmotivating and not very helpful at all.

What you should be doing instead is just going ahead and making a start, i.e. do 20 minutes and build from there rather than thinking about the hours ahead. Another way to look at this example would be to make a start by putting a plan together and then focus on one paragraph at a time, and so on.

Alternatively, as suggested in Chapter 6, you can also use the Traffic Light Method to break tasks down. You can start your work by doing one part and then, over the time you have, chip away at the rest.

By using some of the suggestions in this chapter, you should start to get your work done in the timeframe given and, in turn, avoid getting stressed, anxious or overwhelmed when it comes to completing your schoolwork.

CHAPTER 9

Completing tasks to the best of your ability

What does it mean to have 'finished' your work? Often a lot more than most students think! Working on a task through to completion, along with putting in the best possible effort you can, are valuable skills that will not only help you hit the mark with your schoolwork, but will set you up in the future when you go on to further studies or into the workforce.

Students might rush through their work in order to get it out of the way so they can do other things that they would rather be spending their time on. Unfortunately, when you adopt this approach, the output or quality of the work is usually much lower than if you put in the necessary time and effort – and you can make more mistakes.

How to complete work to the best of your ability

As noted previously, start with an estimate of the time you are likely to need to complete a task, to act as a guide. That way, you can plan ahead and find the time in your day to do this work.

Ensure you understand, and are clear what is required of, the task; if not, follow up with your teacher or a classmate as soon as possible. You should refer to outlines and/or rubrics provided as these usually contain all the necessary details. Continually refer to these as you work on the task as they will help to keep you on track.

Prior to handing in a task, you should also always look at the rubric and crosscheck that everything has been completed. In an ideal world, this will be done at least three days prior to allow for anything missed or to give additional time that might be needed to complete a task.

One strategy you might like to adopt, when you have a task where it might be conducive to do so, is to provide or discuss with your teacher your plan, then submit a draft before handing in the final task. That way, you can seek and incorporate feedback along the way – it can also give you the confidence and peace of mind that you are on track. This approach will likely also help you to submit a better-quality piece of work and, ultimately, get a better result.

I know it can be tempting to just complete a task to get it done and over with. However, by doing this, you are not taking the necessary time needed, and you are unlikely to get a good result. In my experience, a student is usually given a mark that reflects the quality of their work rather than on how quickly it was completed. The same can be said for assessments like exams – students should use all the time available to ensure the best success for them.

Don't you think you will feel better when you can take pride in your efforts and results knowing you did the best you can? Wouldn't it be better for you to feel like this than getting a lower grade just because you rushed to get it done? Adopting the first approach will also set you up with better skills that will be transferable into further studies or into the workforce in due course. A strong work ethic is something that is a valuable skill for you to have now and continue to develop.

Avoiding perfectionism

Unfortunately, for some students, the desire to get work perfect can add an additional complexity to the process when completing tasks. While it might feel good to want to get something perfect, it is actually likely to be more of a hindrance than anything else.

Perfectionism is something that appears to be becoming increasingly common. Students seem to be developing self-defeating thoughts and behaviours, which are often associated with high standards and unrealistic goals.

As a student it is OK to set high standards, however, the relentless pursuit of perfectionism can often impact on getting work done and can also affect other aspects of one's life. It is important for students to realise they can still achieve without having to be 'perfect'. In actual fact, there is no such thing as 'perfect'; it is often something that a person creates in their own mind that they are striving for and can be quite unrealistic. Perfection doesn't exist and it is a big enemy of time, i.e. spending too long on tasks or putting things off until you feel perfect or motivated to make a start.

The other results of this approach include getting frustrated, wasting time, spending too long on tasks, procrastinating and getting stressed and anxious.

One way to deal with perfectionist tendencies is to only focus on getting something completed. And then, if there is additional time available, you can work on the task for a bit longer. It is certainly much better to have it completed, knowing it is done, than to potentially still be striving for completion with perfectionism getting in the way. If this is something you experience, try and take the additional pressure you put on yourself by keeping it simple, completing the task and not overthinking it.

CHAPTER 10

Being a good self-advocate

Hand in hand with organisation and time management for students is being a good self-advocate. You might ask yourself, 'what does that actually mean?' Let me unpack this for you.

What is self-advocating?

As a student or teen, it is:

- Learning how to speak up and communicate for yourself
- Being able to make decisions by yourself
- Being able to learn information and ensure you understand it
- Recognising when you need further information, help or assistance to fill in any gaps or complete your knowledge
- Understanding and knowing expectations
- Knowing who can support you at school and in life
- Being able to problem-solve and knowing how best to deal with any potential roadblocks that get in the way
- Actually going about seeking what it is you need

Connecting with your teachers is crucial to your learning and studies at school. It is important that you are not afraid to ask them for help. They are there, in most instances, to assist as required.

Self-advocating is a key life skill which, along with organisation and time management, is useful in developing independence. By being a good self-advocate, you will also save yourself time in the long run through being more organised ahead of time and by staying on top of your learning, therefore, being more effective and productive overall.

I am sure you have noticed those students in class who are always asking questions, getting involved in discussions or clarifying what they need to do. It is often these students who tend to get better marks as a result of adopting this approach.

Why it is important to seek help as you learn

As a student, when you learn something new it is important to ensure you understand the concept/s or information at the time of learning. This is the time to consolidate and build your knowledge to increase the chances of the information moving from your working memory to your long-term memory, and be there when you need to recall it during a test, assessment or exam.

Unfortunately, many students leave this until much later when they have moved on to another topic or even prior to an exam or test, and therefore decrease their chances of recall when they need it most. It can become the 'illusion of knowing' something, when in fact you actually don't know it at all!

The key message is: if you don't understand something as you are learning it, seek help as soon as possible!

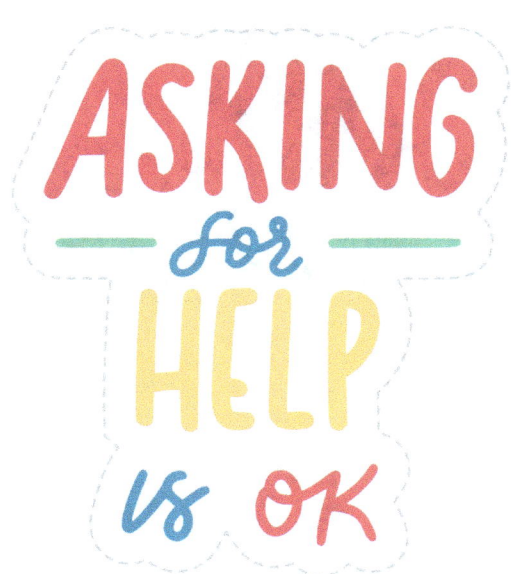

Don't try and do it all by yourself

Too often students say they feel they want to work something out by themselves or don't want to impact on a teacher's time. In my experience, while there are merits for taking the initiative in trying to do something yourself, it can often take much longer and become more stressful at times.

What you would rather do: spend 15 to 30 minutes (or longer) trying to figure something out, or ask your teacher a question that might take less than five minutes to answer? My advice is the latter of the two options, which is a more effective and productive use of your time.

How do you be a good self-advocate?

I appreciate that asking for help can sometimes be scary or daunting. Often students realise they don't understand something and then struggle with how to ask the teacher for what it is they need assistance with.

There are actually many ways you can do this; you need to find what will work best for you. Here are a few ideas that you might like to consider putting into practice:

1. Putting your hand up in class – this is often the quickest option but not the only one, and some people don't feel confident or comfortable doing this.
2. Touching base with the teacher when they walk around during a lesson/class or approaching them at their desk when appropriate during the lesson.
3. Catching the teacher at the start or end of the class.
4. Making a time with your teacher to see them outside of class at another time.
5. Emailing your question to the teacher during or after class.

If you are not quite sure what to say or how to actually ask about something, then these tips might help:

- Just saying something like you don't understand is not really enough for your teacher to help you – try to be clear on what part or what it is you don't understand.
- Use phrases like:
    - 'I understand everything up to this point, but then wasn't clear after that'
    - 'I am not sure why...'

- 'I understand..., but I don't understand...'
- 'Something isn't making sense, but I have tried and I can't quite figure out what I am missing. Can you please help?'
- 'I have attempted some of the homework questions, but I am struggling to complete them. Can you please go through the key concepts again with me?'

Finally, make sure you always thank your teacher for their time and effort in helping you.

CHAPTER 11

The feedback loop

Now that you have managed to learn and understand what it means to be organised and manage your time, it is important that you also review your progress periodically.

As a student, you need to continue to learn and reflect from past experiences and evolve and change accordingly to improve and make things easier so that you are more productive the next time round. This is what is often referred to as 'the feedback loop'.

Self-reflection is an essential skill that, with regular practice, ensures you continue to be effective at both your organisation and time management at school and in other areas of your life. It is how we learn and what we do across all of the points discussed so far in this book that enables us to continue to learn, improve and grow.

This needs to be ongoing and altered along our journey – there is no set time or place for this, but something that needs to be incorporated either as we go or at set points in time.

Without reflecting, we often just continue to follow the same habits, which could be helpful or not, or a mix of both. It is important to take the time and a step back to review what is or isn't working for you, whether that's in one particular area or across many areas.

Learning from teacher feedback

As a student, it is not only important to reflect on your habits, but also on the actual work you are undertaking, and incorporate feedback from teachers. This could be comments given in person or on a task, marks in an assessment/exam or general feedback discussed in class.

Reflecting on this feedback is also an ongoing process that you should be doing regularly. Basically, it is a good habit to begin reflecting on every piece of work you do during the school year. It is a good idea to reflect both on what you have done well and also when things didn't quite go to plan. Doing this will put you in good stead to keep learning and improving your results moving forward. Once you become aware of the feedback, then you need to take the steps to make the necessary changes with the next piece of work, task or in a test or exam. Don't you think this would be a better approach than to keep making the same mistakes over and over again?

Here are three simple questions students should ask themselves regularly when it comes to their work:

1. What is working?
2. What isn't working?
3. What is next? What changes do I need to make?

When you reflect on 'what is next', you are asking yourself to make a choice and to plan how you will move forward with the information you have been given. By doing this, you are creating a self-awareness, and then the next step is to ensure you learn as well as put into practice the necessary changes. Students need to ask themselves, 'how will I use the information I have learned in the future?' If you are not entirely sure what you can do with the feedback and how best to learn from it, speak up and ask your teacher for advice. Remember, they are there to help you and appreciate a student who is proactive and willing to keep learning and improving.

A student will often ask, 'why do I need to do this if I got a good result?' It is equally as important to spend time reflecting on this as when you don't do as well as you expected. The reason for this is that by self-reflecting you can then ensure you replicate this time and time again in the future.

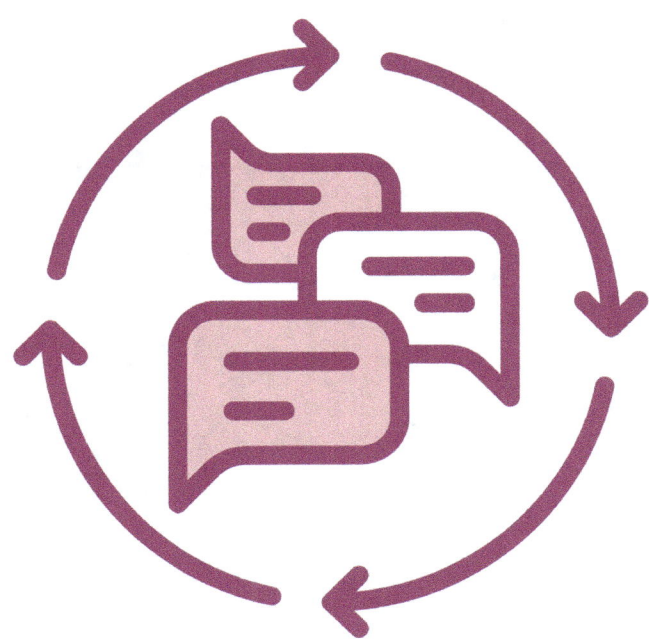

Unfortunately, students often have a tendency to put off the self-reflecting process to a later stage or even just before an assessment or exam. This can be too late as it is more effective to undertake at the time of learning when the information is still relatively fresh in your brain. By doing it at that time, it will increase your chances of building upon and consolidating your knowledge.

Let me ask you now that you know this: why wouldn't you take the time to undertake regular self-reflection and set yourself up for continued growth and success? Please be open to making the time to continue to learn and improve as it is another useful life skill to adopt for your studies and then to take into your future career.

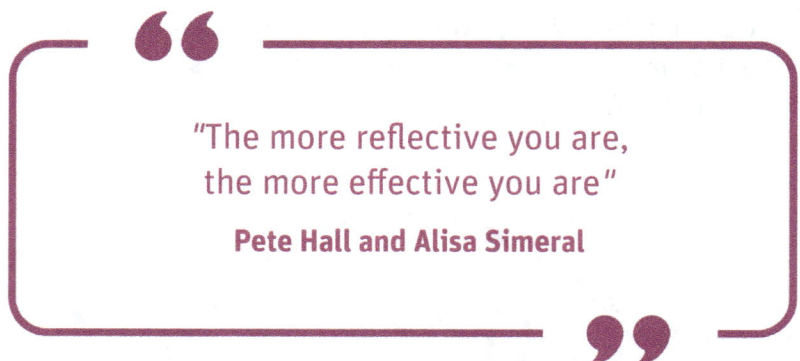

"The more reflective you are, the more effective you are"

Pete Hall and Alisa Simeral

CHAPTER 12
Additional learning challenges

We all use our executive functions (introduced in Chapter 2), which basically help us to 'get stuff done'. Our executive functions help us to:

- Think and plan ahead
- Juggle multiple tasks at once
- Break down tasks
- Prioritise tasks
- Remember key information
- Keep our emotions regulated
- Feel comfortable and manage social situations
- Manage interruptions and distractions
- And the list goes on... you get the picture

We have already addressed many of the above skills and strategies when it comes to managing your time and being organised. The reason for dedicating a chapter to this is that all young people are still in the process of developing their executive functions, and some students can experience greater challenges with theirs. The part of the brain that controls executive function can be less developed than others of the same age. It is certainly not related to intelligence or laziness, but it can impact one's learning, motivation and behaviour.

If you have been diagnosed with one of the following neurological or learning differences, you might find executive function extra challenging:

- **ADHD** can cause difficulty with focus, emotional responses and controlling your actions.
- **Autism** can cause difficulties with managing time, controlling thoughts and actions, remembering things and social interactions.
- **Auditory Processing Disorder** means that your brain has trouble interpreting what you hear.
- **Dyslexia** means that your brain has difficulty recognising and interpreting written words.
- **Dysgraphia** means that your brain has difficulty writing.

Please note there are many other diagnoses, not listed above, that can also impact one's executive functions.

With such diagnoses, students can experience extra challenges with things such as:

- Following directions
- Adjusting to changes in routine
- Switching from one task to another (transition)
- Remembering what you have just heard or read
- Keeping track of your belongings
- Adapting to social situations
- Staying emotionally in control

The good news is that executive function is a skill set that can be developed, and there are additional practices that you and those around you can put in place to help.

Most students do as well as they can, which means that if you are struggling, you may just need a few extra tools. Some of these tools will rely on others to support and guide you towards being able to manage more independently and confidently.

Some additional strategies to assist other than what you have already read about might be:

Reviewing your specific challenges

By being aware of what your key challenges might be, and understanding the problem you might be trying to solve, you will be able to begin to come up with solutions to help.

It can be useful to sit down with your parents and/or teacher to discuss some of the challenges, and work together on potential tools and strategies specific to you that you might be able to use.

Using checklists and reminders

These can be helpful to keep track of steps in a process that you might need to follow. Sometimes the steps are not obvious, and by having them noted down can make the task less daunting and achievable. Having a checklist in place can also help to minimise both the mental and emotional load.

Sometimes the checklists might be standard/routine steps, and other times they might need to be developed and planned for to help with a specific task.

Adjusting to transitions

Think through the shifts you will be making between activities in your day, for example, 'First I will..., followed by..., then...'

Another useful transition tool that can help is, where practical, to stay after school and complete work in the library or in another space. This allows you to complete work while still in school mode and avoid having to come home and then transition back to completing work after having a break.

Using assistive technology

There are many different tools available; here are some examples:

- Voice to text
- Text to voice
- Timers and reminders
- Headphones to block out noise
- Apps to assist with note taking, and so on...

Such tools can help to not only organise your thoughts, but also to help you to focus, stay on task, be more productive and complete work on time.

Body doubling

This basically means for a student to be completing a task in the presence of another person. It is the other person's job to help anchor the student to the present moment and task, help them get started, keep them focused and reduce distractions.

So, rather than trying to complete work at a desk in one's bedroom, it might be better to go and sit next to a parent in their office, or at the kitchen table while they are completing their work so that you can focus on what you need to get done.

Using incentives

Establish these at the outset of a task and then, when a particular task is completed, you have an activity you enjoy doing to look forward to, i.e. playing a computer game, watching a series on a streaming service, meeting or chatting with friends.

These are only some of the many tools and strategies available, and if you are a student who has executive function challenges, you or your parents might also like to do some additional research into what else might be available.

Note: many of the above might also be useful tools and strategies for any students – with executive function challenges or not – to adopt if they work to help you to be better organised and on top of what you need to achieve. It is all about finding what will work for you.

CHAPTER 13

Independence and self-management

Most students want to develop their own independence, and planning can certainly help you to demonstrate to both your teachers and parents that you have everything under control. That doesn't mean that from time to time you can't seek guidance and support, as that, too, can assist, particularly when it might be a busy period, or you find yourself getting a little behind.

Part of being independent is also taking responsibility for your own learning. To help you with this, it is also important for you to know what the expectations are at all times with what you need to do. If you are unsure, just ask your teacher or parents for guidance (see Chapter 10).

As you move through secondary school, each year level will come with increased expectations on you as a student. This will mean that you need to continue to keep trying new things, take on more responsibility, make decisions by yourself and ultimately manage more and more by yourself. By doing all of this, you will be able to tackle tasks and challenges that come your way, and grow in confidence as you do. This is all part of growing up and an essential part of becoming an adult.

The ultimate goal in becoming independent is to be self-sufficient and empower you to be able to navigate through your own journey in life.

So, what is next?

Congratulations if you have read this book through from start to finish, or maybe you just read bits and pieces and a few key chapters.

In an ideal world, you will now go and adopt every single tip, tool and strategy included in this book and put it into practice. In reality, and based on my experience, this will not be the case, nor is it likely to work if you try and do it all at once.

However, I do advise that, as a start, you pick out one to three key things to do now and focus solidly on these becoming part of your regular routine and create new habits.

From there, you might like to then pick a few more to incorporate and work on, and so on.

Organisational skills don't just happen; they take practice, like most things in life, in order for you to get better and for them to be helpful to you.

Remember that having balance is key to managing all of the above. It is important for you to find the right balance that will work for you between your academic and personal life.

I wish you all the best for the remainder of your secondary school journey, and then into your next chapter – whether that be a gap year, further studies or into the workforce. There are many different opportunities ahead, and hopefully many of these practical tools, tips and strategies will help and guide you for many years to come.

www.ingramcontent.com/pod-product-compliance
Lightning Source LLC
Chambersburg PA
CBHW070327120526
44590CB00017B/2831